shamanic
journeying

Sandra Ingerman

shamanic journeying

A Beginner's Guide

SOUNDS TRUE

Sounds True, Inc., Boulder, CO 80306
© 2004, 2008 Sandra Ingerman

Cover photo and drum by Terry Keepers, Shamanic Arts Studio,
shamanicartsstudio.com

First Published 2004
Printed in Canada

ISBN 978-1-59179-943-6

20 19 18 17 16 15 14 13 12

Audio learning programs by Sandra Ingerman from Sounds True:
The Beginner's Guide to Shamanic Journeying
The Soul Retrieval Journey
Miracles for the Earth

Contents

Introduction

When many of us think of the word "shaman," it brings to mind a spiritual healer steeped in secret knowledge and mysterious powers. So how did an ordinary girl from Brooklyn get involved in shamanism back in the 1980s?

In 1980, I was attending the California Institute of Integral Studies, where I was getting my master's degree in counseling psychology. For financial reasons, I had to work sixty hours a week—and I was taking twelve credits a quarter—so I was always looking for easy credits. One day I was in the office at school, and a friend walked in and told me that a man was flying out from Connecticut to teach a weekend workshop on something called shamanism. He did not know what the workshop involved, but he told me that I could get two easy credits by taking it. I immediately signed up—without even looking at what the required reading was. The workshop began on Halloween of 1980.

The man flying in from Connecticut turned out to be Dr. Michael Harner, anthropologist and author of *The Way of the Shaman,* who is known for having revived the tradition of shamanic journeying in modern Western culture. While researching his book, Dr. Harner made a critical discovery that became the basis of his widespread teaching in the West. He found that the shamanic journey is a practice common to all shamans and cultures throughout history, regardless of their geography or cultural differences.

During a shamanic journey, the shaman goes into an altered state of consciousness to journey outside of time and space into what Carlos Castenada called non-ordinary reality—or what I think of as a parallel universe. Typically, the shaman listens to some form of rhythmic percussion, which carries the soul into non-ordinary reality. In these journeys, the shaman retrieves information from helping spirits who make themselves available in non-ordinary reality for healing help and to provide information for patients, family, and their community.

During the weekend workshop, I learned that the practice of shamanic journeying can be used by anyone today in order to get answers to personal questions, to learn different healing methods, to help others in the community, and to work on world and global issues. As soon as I met my helping spirit during my first journey, I realized that this practice would not only help me face the challenges in my life, but would also further my personal growth and evolution. Since then, in concert with my background in psychotherapy, my goal has been to find the best way to apply and share this powerful, ancient technique.

The practice of shamanic journeying is a way for us to feel personally empowered in our lives. It provides us with a way to have direct revelation and is a simple approach for accessing spiritual guidance. It is a way to get us out of our heads as well as to expand our awareness and consciousness.

When we begin to learn that we have the ability to problem solve for ourselves, it raises our self-esteem in a grounded way. Going to meet our helping spirits makes us feel valued and connected to the spirit that lives in all things. We feel loved by the power of the universe, and we never feel alone again.

In working with the helping spirits, we learn the true definition of power. True power is being able to use our energy to create transformation for ourselves, others, and the planet.

Shamanic journeying is a joyful path to regaining the knowledge of how to bring our lives back into a place of harmony and balance. It helps us to wake up to our full creative potential. As we do this, our lives change in a way that brings good health and well-being to ourselves and others. I have watched people who have been depressed wake up to the joy of life. People have started dancing and singing after a lifetime of repressing their creative spark. I have watched people build their lives back up after suffering debilitating illness and personal loss. I have watched people get their "voice" back. We just need to have the desire and an open heart to do this work. Everyone can journey and open to the new dimensions of life that the spirits are waiting to show us.

It is important to understand that I will not be training you to become a shaman. Traditionally, it is not typical for someone to volunteer for the role of shaman or to self-identify as a shaman. Rather, someone is chosen by "the spirits" to become a shaman and to act in the service of his or her community. In shamanic cultures, it is actually considered bad luck to call yourself a shaman, because this is seen as bragging, and the shamanic view about power is that if you brag about having it, you will lose it. Instead, your community recognizes you as a shaman based on the successful results that you achieve for the benefit of your clients and the greater community.

In *Shamanic Journeying: A Beginner's Guide*, you will learn one of the most fundamental techniques used by shamans worldwide to connect with spiritual helpers, to access personal spiritual guidance and healing, to help others and the planet, and to reconnect with nature and its cycles and rhythms: the shamanic journey. This practice is designed to give you direct access to your own spiritual guidance. I believe that the times we live in call for each of us to develop tools for resolving our own problems, tools that enable us to become more empowered and resourceful.

Many of you will use this method for your own personal healing, growth, and evolution. After extensive practice, some of you will be guided to begin using this work to help others in your community and in your work to help the planet. This program is designed to provide you with an introduction to the technique of journeying in such a way that your own destiny with it can unfold. The accompanying CD contains three drumming sessions to help you get started with your journey practice. Once you have completed reading *Shamanic Journeying: A Beginner's Guide*, you will be ready to use the CD as an accompaniment to your journeys into non-ordinary reality.

Shamanism: The Path of Direct Revelation

Shamanism is the earliest spiritual practice known to humankind, dating back tens of thousands of years. Although the word "shaman" is a Siberian word for a spiritual healer, shamanism has also been practiced in parts of Asia, Europe, Africa, Australia, Greenland, and native North and South America throughout history. The fact that the practice has survived and thrived for tens of thousands of years speaks to the potency of the work.

One of the beautiful aspects of the shamanic journey is the principle of direct revelation. The practice of shamanic journeying helps us to part the veils between the seen and unseen worlds and access information and energies that can help awaken us and restore us to wholeness. A shaman is a man or woman who interacts directly with spirits to address the spiritual aspects of illness, perform soul retrievals, divine information, help the spirits of deceased people cross over, and perform a variety of ceremonies for the community. Shamans have taken on many roles in tribal communities. They have acted as healers, doctors, priests, psychotherapists, mystics, and storytellers.

Traditionally, the practice of shamanism has focused on practical results achieved by the shaman. In a traditional shamanic culture, there was either a single individual or a few people in the community acting in the role of shaman. The shaman would be consulted by hunters and gatherers in the tribe to identify food sources. If the shaman were unable to accurately divine the location of food, the tribe would not survive. Shamans were also expected to perform healings for members of the community. Once again, the survival of the tribe was largely dependent on the shaman's spiritual abilities.

Shamanism teaches us that everything that exists is alive and has a spirit, and that we are joined with the earth and all of life via our spiritual interconnectedness. Just as quantum physics describes a field of energy that connects all of life, shamans also speak of a web of life that connects everything. In modern culture, many of us feel a deep longing to experience our unity with this web of life and to heal our sense of isolation. When we travel to non-ordinary reality in our shamanic journeys, we learn how to communicate with the spirit of the trees, plants, animals, insects, birds, fish, reptiles, and rocks, as well as the spirit of the elements of earth, air, water, and fire. We directly experience the web of life.

As we are a part of nature, we have a deep need to reconnect with nature's cycles and rhythms. Imagine how exhausting it would be to walk against the flow of a river every day of your life. In truth, we have disconnected from the cycles and rhythms of the moon and the seasons, and often we do walk against the flow of the river of life. I believe this is partly the cause of such ailments as chronic fatigue, depression, and a host of other illnesses, both psychological and physical, that are so common today. The helping spirits have a great deal to teach us about restoring balance and harmony into our lives by reconnecting with nature's cycles and by living in unity with the natural world.

Within the practice of shamanism, there are a variety of ceremonies performed for honoring and working with the cycles of nature and the cycles in our own lives, as well as for reading omens and interpreting dreams—all of which provide insight, healing, and empowerment. Shamanism can also teach us the value of having a regular spiritual practice and the value of being in service to others, which brings a genuine sense of meaning and purpose to our lives. Finally, shamanism enables us to access powerful forces to help us create the world we want to live in—for ourselves and for others.

Shamans heal emotional and physical illness by working with the spiritual aspect of illness. The traditional role of the shaman has been to perform ceremonies. After tens of thousands of years, traditional shamans are still part of community life and practice in Siberia, Asia, Australia, Africa, and North and South America. The technique of shamanic journeying that you will learn in this book is just one of the ceremonies shamans use to establish communication with the spirit world.

There are three common causes of illness in the shaman's view. First, a person may have lost his or her power, causing depression, chronic illness, or a series of misfortunes. In this case, the shaman journeys to restore that person's lost power. Or a person may have lost part of his or her soul or essence, causing soul loss, which sometimes occurs during an emotional or physical trauma, such as accidents, surgery, abuse, the trauma of war, being in a natural disaster, or other traumatic circumstances. This soul loss results in dissociation, post-traumatic stress syndrome, depression, illness, immune deficiency problems, addictions, unending grief, or coma. It is the role of the shaman to track down the parts that have fled and been lost due to trauma by performing a soul retrieval ceremony. The third cause of illness from a shaman's perspective would be any spiritual blockages or negative energies that a client has taken on due to the loss of his or her power or soul. These spiritual blockages also cause illness, usually in a localized area of the body. It is the role of the shaman to extract and remove these harmful energies from the body.

Other ceremonies performed by shamans include welcoming children into the world, performing marriages, and helping people at the time of death transition from body to spirit. Shamans also work to encourage the growth of crops, help people to interpret dreams, and advise people who are experiencing trouble. Shamans are in charge of initiation ceremonies conducted around transitions from one phase of life into another, such as initiating children into adulthood. Shamans tell stories about the meaning of life and show us how the spirits can help us find our way when we feel lost in our life circumstances. They can remove spells or dark energies, and read the tenor of the community, picking up disharmony and imbalance. They create ceremonies to mourn the loss of a member of the community. Shamans also read signs and omens to choose auspicious times to undertake activities such as hunting and celebrations.

Shamans understand the cycles of nature—the cycles of the seasons and moons, and how the stars move across the sky. They read the signs that come with these changes and movements. They communicate with the weather spirits and maintain harmony and balance in their communities.

Typically, there would be more than one shaman in a community. Different shamans would be known for their spiritual areas of expertise. For instance, some shamans would be known for their great successes in particular healing ceremonies such as soul retrievals, while others are known for their divination abilities.

Over time, the practice of shamanism has adapted in response to different cultural needs and the changing needs of the times. Currently, there is a dramatic revival of shamanism in the West, with a wide range of people integrating shamanic practices into their lives, including students, housewives, teachers, psychotherapists, lawyers, nurses, doctors, politicians, and scientists. I believe that one of the main reasons for this revival is that people want to be able to access their own spiritual guidance. We want to stop giving away our power to socially acceptable authority figures. We know that we are the only ones who truly have the power to change our own lives.

The Three Worlds

According to the shamanic view, there is an invisible reality beyond the physical world that is accessible through shamanic journeying. In Celtic shamanism, this unseen reality is known as the "Other World." In the Australian aboriginal tradition, the unseen world is known as the "Dreamtime." Many shamanic traditions believe that unseen reality is divided into three separate worlds: the Lower World, the Upper World, and the Middle World. Each world has distinct qualities, including particular gateways or entryways and a recognizable landscape. In this introduction, I would like to present each of these three worlds, including their distinct gateways and differences in landscape.

The Lower World is sometimes known by the term "Underworld," although for some people that term can have a negative connotation. The landscape in the Lower World tends to be earthy, filled with mountains, deserts, dense jungles, and forests. When I teach journeying, I recommend that people begin by journeying to the Lower World.

To journey to the Lower World, you begin by visualizing a location in nature that you have visited in ordinary reality and have a clear memory of, and you use that spot to travel down into the earth. Traditional ways of entering the Lower World include climbing down the roots of a tree, traveling down the center of a volcano, through a hole in the ground, into an entrance of a cave, or through a body of water, such as a lake, stream, river, or waterfall. Any way that you can see yourself in a specific location in nature using a natural opening to travel into the earth is fine. If you do not have a clear picture of a natural opening, you can see yourself traveling down into the earth on an elevator or in a subway if that is easier for you.

People often experience a transitional phase once they have entered their opening that appears as a tunnel leading them into the Lower World. A literary example of that transition can be found in the story of *Alice in Wonderland*, where Alice descends into another realm through a magical tunnel. Eventually, you come out into the light, and the landscape of your surroundings becomes clear. This is the Lower World.

In contrast, many people experience the Upper World as very ethereal. The light tends to be bright, although the spectrum of colors can include everything from soft pastels to complete darkness. The landscapes in the Upper

World can be quite varied, and you might find yourself in a crystal city or simply in the clouds. When you are in the Upper World, it is common to feel as if you are standing on something, although you can no longer feel the earth beneath your feet.

To journey to the Upper World, you want to begin by seeing yourself at a particular location in nature that will help you travel upward. Some shamans use the Tree of Life, climbing up the branches into the Upper World. Other traditional ways of traveling into the Upper World are climbing up a rope or ladder, jumping from the top of a mountain, rising up on a tornado or a whirlwind, climbing over a rainbow, going up the smoke of a fire or through a chimney, or finding a bird to take you. Today, some people travel to the Upper World on a hot-air balloon, others just float up to it, and others ask their power animal or guardian spirit to carry them up. Any way you can get to the Upper World is fine.

There will be a transition you pass through that will indicate you have entered the Upper World. For some people it is a cloud layer or a layer of fog. This will be a transition, not a barrier, like in the story of "Jack and the Beanstalk," where he climbs up the beanstalk and has to go through a cloud layer before entering a new world. Similarly, in *The Wizard of Oz,* Dorothy travels to another world on a tornado, which is a common experience in shamanism. In fact, there are many children's stories that speak of traveling to non-ordinary reality that are consistent with actual practices in traditional shamanism.

When you have passed through this transition, you will arrive at the first level of the Upper World. If you are still seeing planets and stars as you journey upward, you have not yet reached the Upper World. Again, you will know that you are in the Upper World because of the sensation of having passed through a permeable threshold of some kind, after which the landscape will change.

Although many shamanic traditions view the Lower and Upper Worlds as containing a definite number of levels, many of us have found that there is an unlimited number of levels, because the universe itself is unlimited. Each level will have something special to teach you, and it is up to you to explore them.

The Middle World is the spiritual dimension of our physical world. Middle World journeying is a method for communicating with the spirits that live in all things present in physical reality. Shamans classically journey to the Middle World to find lost and stolen objects, to commune with nature, or to do long-distance healing work. Another great journey to take in the Middle World is a journey to the moon to ask about the moon's different cycles and phases and how they affect your feelings and behavior. In this way, you can learn how to make changes in your life that are in alignment with your natural cycles, giving you an increased sense of well-being. You can also speak to the sun, the stars, and the elements in nature, each of which has much to teach us about how to restore balance in our lives.

When you journey in the Middle World, you are in present time, traveling through our physical landscape. Simply see yourself walking out your front door and stepping into your garden, or traveling through space very quickly to look for something you have lost or to reach a more distant destination. You might take a Middle World journey to meet with the plants, trees, and rocks where you live, to learn more about them and come into balance with them. George Washington Carver was a very respected botanist who said he gained knowledge about cultivating plants from walking through the forest and talking to them. Shamans have always talked to the animals and the plants within and outside their journeys to learn about nature, cycles, rhythms, and the environment in which they live. However, do not rely exclusively on your journeys in the Middle World to connect with nature. You also want to spend time outdoors communing with nature, and hopefully your journeys will inspire you to do so.

The Middle World can be a little complicated to work with, as there are many different types of spirits who live there. Some of the spirits who live there are deceased souls who have suffered traumatic deaths and have not successfully crossed over to the other side. Some of these spirits may not even know that they are dead. To assist them, you would need to receive further training than what this program can provide. In fact, there is a whole area of shamanic training called psychopomp work, which includes methods for helping souls complete their crossing-over process. However, it is fine to journey to speak to the spirit of a tree, a plant, a river, or the wind, or to meet the fairies, devas, and elves that live in the Middle World.

During your journeys, you can choose to travel to the Lower World, the Upper World, or the Middle World. You can choose to engage in conversation with the spirits that you encounter, or you can simply move on. It is important to understand as you undertake shamanic journeying that you have complete control of where you go and whom you talk to. Part of the exploration and wonder of non-ordinary reality is to discover the qualities that go with the different territories—including a variety of landscapes—and what spirits live there. Our helping spirits have the ability to travel between the worlds and can accompany us on our journeys for transportation and support, regardless of where we journey.

Finally, there are no set rules about what people should experience when they journey to each world, although I will describe some common experiences to help you understand the differences between the worlds. However, it is vital that you trust your own experience—rather than trying to replicate someone else's—and that you remember that each person's experience is equally valid.

Power Animals and Teachers

As your shamanic journey practice deepens, you will find yourself meeting many different helping spirits. There are two main types of helping spirits that shamans consult and work with in their journeys: power animals, also known as guardian spirits, and teachers in human form. Power animals and teachers are found in both the Lower and Upper Worlds.

Typically, you will have one or two main power animals, guardian spirits, or teachers who will work with you on an ongoing basis on the core issues in your life. In addition, some power animals and teachers will share specific lessons and skills with you and then move on, with new helping spirits appearing to take their place. With time, you will learn to trust your helping spirits—both your primary ones and your temporary ones—and rely on them for help and guidance. They will accompany you on your journeys throughout life.

Power Animals and Guardian Spirits

In shamanic cultures, it is believed that when we are born, the spirit of at least one animal volunteers itself to protect and guide us throughout our life—this is our power animal. When a person is consciously aware of his or her power animal, it is possible to communicate with it directly and ask them for help and guidance within a shamanic journey. When a person is not conscious of his or her power animal, they are still receiving invisible support, although they may not be aware of it. Some people report having whole teams of animals around them, but it is more common for someone to have one or two main power animals, with other helping animal spirits being more peripheral.

Your power animal represents the entire species of the animal that is protecting and helping you. For example, you do not have the spirit of a specific eagle, kangaroo, or squirrel protecting you. Rather, you have the protection of the spirit of the entire species of eagle, kangaroo, or squirrel. It is very common to have a mythological creature as a power animal, such as Pegasus or a unicorn. You can also have an extinct animal volunteering itself as your power animal, since the spirit of an animal species is eternal. Therefore, it is not unusual for someone to have a type of dinosaur, such as stegosaurus, as his or her power animal.

Today there are many books about the spiritual symbolism of different animals. Since shamanism is based on direct revelation, it is best not to rely on someone else's interpretation of the animals that you encounter on your journeys. If you do not recognize the species of animal that you encounter, either by their appearance or their behaviors, you can refer to a resource book about animals in order to identify the animal. However, consulting a book on the symbology of a particular animal spirit will not help you discover the unique spiritual qualities the animal is offering to you. To uncover that information, it is best ask the animal directly what gifts, qualities, and support it is bringing to you.

In my workshops, I often hear students report that on a journey an elephant volunteered itself to them as a power animal. When asked what he had to teach them, many students have told me that the elephant replied, "I am trying to teach you to lighten up." However, you will not find that the elephant represents a message to "lighten up" in any symbology book!

I personally received a very powerful teaching about this in the late 1980s, when I was doing quite a bit of traveling and teaching. Often, people who attend my workshops and lectures bring a gift for me. However, there was a particular period of time when I received a strong message through a series of gifts that I did not, at first, understand. To begin with, I arrived at a workshop and received two gifts that represented owl—an owl feather and an owl fetish. Fetishes come from the Zuni tribe and are little carved statues imbued with the power of a particular animal.

I thought that it was strange to receive two gifts that belonged to owl, as I had never talked about owl being a helping spirit for me. But that was just the beginning! For the next month, gifts that represented owl kept appearing. The barrage of owl gifts culminated with a handmade owl mask, which one of my students had made for me. There was obviously a message in this, but I did not know what it was.

I journeyed to my main guardian spirit whom I have been working with since 1980. I asked him why so many people were giving me gifts associated with owl and why owl was coming into my life. He responded that owl not only sees in the dark but also has a particular type of radar that I would soon need. Then the journey abruptly ended. As journeys are outside of time, the word "soon" can be far in the distant future, so I did not believe that the reason for owl coming into my life was going to be revealed in the very near future.

A couple of weeks later I was teaching a workshop in St. Louis. The workshop ended Sunday evening, and I had clients who would be coming for sessions with me early Monday morning in Santa Fe, so I had to take a late flight home. At one point during the flight, all the lights went out in the cabin of the plane, and the crew began walking up and down the aisles carrying flashlights. I assumed they were trying to let the passengers sleep.

Shortly thereafter, the pilot made an announcement saying that he bet we were all wondering what was happening. Actually, I had not been thinking about it at all, but now I was suddenly very alert. He said that our plane had an electrical short circuit and that we had no lights—either inside the cabin or on the outside of the plane. In addition, we were about to fly through a lightning storm, and we had no radar to help guide us through.

I immediately thought back to all of the owl-related gifts I had been receiving, and the answer I had been given in my journey a few weeks before when my helping spirit said that owl had a particular type of radar that I was going to need soon. Thankfully, the plane landed safely without any problems and I am certain that owl's presence was part of the reason that we arrived safely that night. It was a profound teaching about how the universe was taking care of me by anticipating the help I would need and providing it for me.

Now, if I had consulted one of the popular symbology books and looked up the spiritual significance of owl, I probably would have found something about transformation—but I certainly would not have gotten anything about radar, or that I was going to need this specific gift from owl in the not-too-distant future. What I learned is that when we do not go back into our own journeys to find the meaning of our power animals and their messages, we often miss the unique lessons they are offering us. Therefore, it is important not to look to others to interpret the spiritual lessons associated with your power animals—that is between you and your power animal. Also, what they have to offer you may not be consistent with your preconceived notions about their particular abilities and skills.

It is also important to be aware of your ideas about the amount of power that different animals hold. I have watched people in workshops get upset because they have squirrel as a power animal instead of something they think of as more mighty and powerful, like bear or eagle. However, in non-ordinary reality, one species of animal does not have more power than another. All power animals have extreme power, and they each have unique and often unexpected lessons to teach us. A mouse has as much power as a lion, but they each have something very different to teach us.

Trees and beings like elves and fairies can also be helping spirits. Since the spirits of trees and beings like elves are not animals, we call them guardian spirits instead. Plants are not usually considered guardian spirits, but are used by shamans around the world for their healing properties.

In shamanic cultures, community life was very important. The process of individuation that we see as so important in our culture today was not important in indigenous cultures, as each individual needed to contribute to the community to ensure its survival. In some cultures, people belonged to certain clans where a power animal volunteered help to the entire group or community of people. Likewise, during my journeys for others, I have found that couples, families, and even organizations and businesses often have a power animal supporting them in non-ordinary reality.

Occasionally, I have found in journeys that some mammals may demonstrate threatening behavior in order to show you how much power they have. It is not unusual to encounter a bear as a power animal that stands up in a threatening fashion in order to express its power. If that occurs, I would suggest that you ask the bear what it has to teach you about strength and power.

There is one source of confusion regarding the appearance of animals in journeys that I would like to address—animals that carry venom and normally sting, poison, or bite humans. Insects such as ants, bees, and spiders can be power animals, although if you perceive them swarming in one area of a body they may be pointing to an illness. For instance, when a shaman goes into an altered state of consciousness and looks into the body of his or her client, he or she might see a reptile showing its fangs, or a localized swarm of ants. Similarly, snakes, lizards, and dragons can be power animals, but if they display their fangs or hiss at you, this may be a sign of illness. There are exceptions when the bite of an animal is meant to transmit power. For example, when I first met the white cobra, which is one of my helping spirits, she bit me on the neck; this was her way of sharing her power and transmitting her healing energies to me. I have met other experienced journeyers who have had the same experience with cobra. The important distinction to make is that the animal that has appeared to you is showing itself as a true helper. For example, some people have a big friendly spider as a power animal. However, this is quite different from seeing thousands of spiders swarming in someone's liver.

In shamanic journeying, your intention lets the spirits know what you are asking to be shown. When embarking on a journey where your intention is to meet a power animal or guardian spirit, that is what you will be shown; not swarms of insects. When the shaman journeys with the intention to be shown the spiritual identity of an illness, sometimes insects or fanged reptiles will appear, alerting the shaman to the location of illness in a client's body.

One final thing to bear in mind is that you do not want to brag about the identity of your power animal. As I said earlier, in shamanism when we brag about our power, we lose it.

Teachers in Human Form

The other types of helping spirits shamans typically work with are called teachers in human form. In a traditional shamanic society, these would be gods and goddesses of that culture, as well as ancestral spirits. Nowadays, people also meet a variety of other teachers, including religious figures such as Jesus, Mary, or Buddha. Some people meet inspirational historical figures such as Einstein or Hildegard von Bingen. Many people report having a deceased relative, such as a grandmother or grandfather, as a teacher. Others work with gods and goddesses, such as Isis, Osiris, and Hermes.

It is important to remain open about the many forms of teachers who present themselves to you. For example, you might find a young child presenting herself as a teacher for you. Or when you are journeying about an issue, you might find a mirror being presented to you, meaning that you are to be your own teacher concerning a particular matter.

I have had the same main guardian spirit since 1980, but I have found other helping spirits who support me with different issues in my life for a while and then move on. There are also power animals around me who help me and provide me with general support, but with whom I do not communicate on a regular basis. I also have had different teachers who have appeared in human form, although my main teacher is Isis, whom I first met in 1986 while I was on a vision quest.

My guardian spirit is the one who does shamanic healing during my journeys for others. He also helps me answer questions in my personal life. Isis answers questions for me personally, and she also helps me when I write my books, when I am teaching workshops, and while I am lecturing at conferences.

As with power animals, teachers are a source of healing and wisdom in our lives. For instance, Nancy, one of my students, had a very profound healing through ongoing work with her teacher. She had experienced abuse as a child and suffered from depression, for which she was taking medication. When she began journeying, she met her teacher, who was King James IV of Scotland. Since Nancy was a schoolteacher, she decided to do some research to learn about the life of King James. She found many books about his life, and through her research she discovered that King James had been abused as a child by his father. She learned that he had healed himself and overcome his early traumas, and she realized she could also be healed. Through reading his story and journeying to him, Nancy finally put her past behind her and has been depression-free and off of antidepressants for years.

Another student, Isabel, was planning to take a vacation with her husband in Hawaii. She journeyed to her teacher and asked if there was anything she needed to know before going on her trip. Her teacher told her to bring rope.

Isabel was understandably surprised by this response, as she was not planning to backpack or go mountain climbing in Hawaii. She told her husband and some friends about the advice she had gotten on her journey, and they just laughed, but she decided to bring rope anyway, and she put some in her daypack. While in Hawaii, Isabel went for a hike on a popular trail with her husband in an area where there had been a lot of rain, which had caused several mudslides. At one point on the trail they slipped and became trapped, and Isabel used the rope to climb to safety.

Similar to the way owl came into my life before I needed owl's help, here is an example of how a helping spirit gave advice to protect someone from a future event. These experiences show us that we are loved and taken care of by our helping spirits.

Relating to Your Helping Spirits

Power animals, guardian spirits, and teachers are known as helping spirits. Sometimes your helping spirits will show themselves to you as tired or sick. It is important to remember that they are spirits—they do not get tired or sick. They might be role-playing your physical or emotional state. They also might be testing you to see if you will offer assistance or love to them. It is a show of loyalty and commitment to be nurturing toward them in light of all that they give you.

Power animals and guardian spirits do not become jealous of each other. Sometimes in a journey you might see two of your power animals fighting. It is important to remember that they are spirits and when they show themselves in a journey as fighting with each other, they are most likely role-playing something going on in your life that you need to look at. Ask them what they are trying to communicate through their behavior so that you can receive the lesson that they are intending for you.

It is important to find a power animal or guardian spirit you can trust who can be your guide through your adventures in non-ordinary reality and who can answer questions for you. If you see or feel a spirit and you are not sure it is a helper to you, you should avoid it, just like you would move around a reptile or insect you did not want to interact with while hiking in the woods. Journeying is very safe, and it is important to learn that you always have full control over where you travel and with which spirits you interact.

Classically, shamans would merge with their power animals and teachers through ritual song and dance. It is considered a generous offering to invite our helping spirits to move through our bodies, as they are disincarnate and unable to experience the pleasure of physical reality themselves. This practice is a way for shamans to connect with the power of their helping spirits and to honor them by allowing them to "dance through" their bodies.

I recommend that you explore how best to honor your helping spirits in your own way. In so doing, you will find that they stay with you for a longer time than if you were to ignore their presence and their attempts to help you in your spiritual life. One way to honor your helping spirits is to write a poem about them or draw a picture of them. Sometimes when I journey in non-ordinary reality, I bring my helping spirits a picnic basket and feed them. During one of these journeys, my intention is simply to give thanks, and I do not ask them any questions or ask for their help. This is my way of saying "thank you" for all of the help that they have given me during my twenty years of journeying.

There is no cross-cultural agreement on the appropriateness of sharing the identity of your helping spirits with others. In some cultures, everyone in the community knows the identity of the protecting spirits of each person. However, I would suggest you journey to your helping spirits and ask them personally what they feel is best. I find some of my helping spirits say it is okay to share their identity with the public, and I write about them and talk about them in my lectures, but my main power animal has told me it is best to keep his identity to myself. On the other hand, it is sometimes beneficial to share the identity of your helping spirits in order to explain your spiritual practice to others, but I recommend that you ask for permission first.

Power animals and teachers live in both the Lower and Upper Worlds. You can do exploratory journeys as part of your shamanic practice to meet different power animals and teachers in different levels of the Lower and Upper Worlds. Power animals and teachers can travel between all the worlds and can accompany you on your shamanic journeys wherever you go. You can also call them into the Middle World when you feel you need their protection or help.

For example, let us say you are feeling nervous about going into a difficult meeting. With a clear intention, call to your power animals and teachers and ask them to be with you during the meeting to help guide you and diminish your anxiety. Or, if you are about to drive on the freeway and you are feeling nervous, you can call to your helping spirits and ask for their protection to help you get home safely.

I use this technique a great deal in my day-to-day life. For example, I am a very nervous flier—and I spend a lot of time traveling on airplanes. When I get on the plane, I do a particular silent meditation to help me feel more at ease. I silently ask that all of my power animals, teachers, and helping spirits join me on the airplane to ensure a safe and smooth flight all the way to my destination. I also ask that the crew and other passengers' power animals, teachers, and helping spirits come forward in order to create a safe and smooth flight for everyone. From a shamanic perspective, everything is alive and has a spirit—so I also call upon the airplane's power animals and helping spirits to be present to ensure a safe flight.

Our relationship with our helping spirits also provides us with protection from the common phenomenon of burnout. Energetically, when you come into close contact with other people, you can "pick up" their feelings and thoughts. You may even have someone "tugging" on your energy because they are in need of support or help. Shamanism gives us ways to be fully present with someone without taking on their suffering on an energetic level—which can lead to burnout as well as illness. In this situation, a classic shamanic practice is to silently ask your power animal or teacher to fill you up with power and strengthen your boundaries before you meet with someone who is in need.

In this way, you are not open to the invisible exchange that occurs on an energetic level, where someone else's material is transferred onto you. You can also use this method before walking into a crowded room or street in order to remain energetically intact.

This technique of calling your helping spirits into the Middle World is not the same as beginning to journey in the middle of your day—or when you are engaged in your ordinary life. There are times when it is appropriate to journey and times when it is not. In fact, traditional shamans perform ceremonies and rituals before journeying and are very deliberate about when they choose to journey into non-ordinary reality to contact their helping spirits. People who cannot follow the discipline of deliberately entering and leaving non-ordinary reality are no longer practicing shamanism—they are entering the world of psychosis. People who are psychotic do not know what world they are in. In contrast, a shaman's journey is always deliberate, purposeful, and intentional.

You will find as you begin to practice journeying on a regular basis that the helping spirits you work with can provide you with all kinds of assistance. Of course you must take responsibility for the choices you make in your life. Your helping spirits will not do everything for you. However, you will find that they can truly support you as you continue moving forward on your soul's path.

Preparing to Journey

Traditionally, shamans created ceremony and ritual around their journeys. They only journeyed with intentionality and purpose. They took time to prepare themselves by singing and dancing in order to clear their minds so they could become "a hollow bone"—a true instrument for the power of the universe.

When you are ready to undertake your first journey, make sure you have a clear intention and purpose for your journey. Even if you just want to explore the Lower World, Middle World, or Upper World, make sure that you are clear that this is your purpose. If you have a question in mind, repeat the question several times. If you just lie down and listen to the drumming without setting an intention, it is possible that you might have a powerful journey, although many people report that when they journey without an intention their journeys are fuzzy and disjointed. The key to all spiritual practice—whether it is shamanic journeying or meditation—is concentration. It is important to learn how to concentrate during your journeys and not to get distracted by mind chatter or the concerns of ordinary life.

It is important for you to determine when the best time of day is for you to journey. You will need to experiment to find the times of day when you can concentrate the best— when you are fresh and your mind is clear, not when your mind is cluttered with a lot of details. Many people report that the best time for them to journey is in the morning before they engage in their lives. Late afternoon is not usually a good time to journey. People often complain that their journeys are fragmented and confusing during this time of day. Some people prefer to journey right before they go to bed at night. I can journey at any time of the day for a client, but when I journey for myself, I tend to have the clearest journeys in the morning before I get pulled out of that quiet after-sleep space into my daily life.

There is no one cross-cultural belief about what kind of diet best supports shamanic journeying. It is true that in many cultures shamans adhere to a special diet before they do certain ceremonies and healing work. You really have to explore what works for you in terms of foods that increase or diminish your ability to focus. Generally, I find that alcohol interferes with maintaining concentration and staying alert in journeys. Also, if you eat a heavy meal before you journey, your body will be focused on digestion and it might be difficult for you to concentrate and stay alert. Some people find that caffeine can help their concentration on a journey, although my experience has been that a little caffeine may help create clear journeys, but too much caffeine can "close the curtains" between you and non-ordinary reality.

I suggest that you find a comfortable, quiet place for your journey where you will not be interrupted. Disconnecting your phone is a useful precaution to take. You can journey lying down or sitting up. Remember that you will have a clearer journey if you are alert, so you might not want to get too comfortable or you might just fall asleep.

Once you have established your spot, you may want to dance, sing, chant, or do some movement exercises to get the oxygen moving through your system. This will also open your heart and help you feel a sense of unity with all of life. Movement, dancing, chanting, and singing help to break down the egoistic barriers that can prevent us from having a clear journey. In addition, the spirits communicate with us through our hearts, and we "see" in our journeys through our hearts. So taking the time to breathe into your heart to allow it to open more fully is beneficial. I teach people who have a hard time concentrating during their journeys to focus on breathing deeply through their hearts, and people report great successes from adding this to their practice. So if you lose your concentration while you are journeying, or if you feel that you are not experiencing anything, make sure you are breathing through your heart. Keep repeating the intention of the journey and what you are asking for until your focus returns and you are back on track.

One of the many definitions of shaman is "one who sees in the dark." It is a lot easier to journey in total darkness. Therefore, some people close the shades and curtains to darken the room. You can also use a blindfold of some sort—such as a bandana, scarf, or eye pillow—to keep the light out of your eyes. Do whatever is most comfortable for you.

Once again, take some deep breaths before you begin and during your journey to facilitate a clear experience. Then, before you start the drumming CD, clarify your intention. Repeat it to yourself as many times as you need in order to be focused and clear about the purpose of your journey. Visualize your starting place in nature through which you will leave to go to the Lower or Upper World. If you are journeying in the Middle World, visualize the doorway through which you will leave.

Remember that you have complete control of where you go, whom you talk to, and when you return from the journey. Journeying is not like a sleeping dream where, unless you have studied lucid dreaming, you are not in control of what is happening to you. If you are having a nightmare, for instance, you are stuck in the nightmare without a way of ending it. This will never be the case during a shamanic journey.

During a shamanic journey, you can choose to go to the Lower World, the Middle World, or the Upper World. You can choose to engage in conversation with a spirit or to move on. You cannot, however, choose what helping spirit volunteers itself to help you, although you can hold the intention that you want to meet a particular helping spirit that you have already met on a previous journey. Allow yourself to be surprised.

The Role of the Drum in Shamanic Journeying

Cross-culturally, most shamans use monotonous or rhythmic drumming to alter their state of consciousness when they journey. There are also traditions that use rattles, sticks, and bells. In Australia the shamans use didgeridoos and click sticks. The Sami people of Lapland and Norway use either drums or monotonous chants called *joiking*. The monotonous sounds generated by these instruments put the shaman into an altered state of consciousness, allowing him or her to successfully journey into the invisible worlds.

Today there are scientific instruments that can measure brain activity during altered states of consciousness. When we are in an ordinary state of consciousness, our brainwaves are in what scientists call a beta state. However, when we listen to monotonous drumming, scientists have discovered that our brainwaves slow down. First they slow down to the alpha state, which signals the beginning state of meditation. Then our brainwaves slow down even more into a theta state. This is the brainwave state in which we do our shamanic journeying—where we can explore the invisible worlds and have contact with our helping spirits.

It is possible to journey without a drum, although by making it a habit to listen to percussion or other music that helps you alter your state of consciousness, you will become more focused and disciplined in your shamanic practice. You may continue to receive spontaneous intuitive insights throughout the day, but it is important to create a routine within your shamanic practice. This ensures that your journeys are clearly separate from the rest of your day.

Certain shamanic traditions include the use of psychotropic plants (hallucinogens), or what some people today call "vision plants." There are many psychotropic plants that are native to the Amazon and other parts of South America that shamans use to heal or to help them divine guidance for their communities. There is also evidence that psychotropic mushrooms and other plants are used cross-culturally for these purposes. Of course, this is a controversial topic that has long been debated among anthropologists.

However, since shamans have also traditionally used drums, rattles, and other forms of percussion in their journeys, I consider drumming and rattling to be the most effective, appropriate, and easily adaptable accompaniment for our culture today. As we continue to rely on the practice of shamanism to help solve the problems of our times, we must make sure the methods we use are appropriate and safe for people today.

Although traditional shamans developed their own drumming rhythms to support their travels into non-ordinary reality, Dr. Michael Harner has found that using one drumbeat is the best way to teach beginners how to journey. Therefore, the enclosed CD uses one monotonous rhythm. During the first twelve-minute drumming track, I begin by doing some whistling and rattling for a few minutes, which will help prepare the space for you. Whistling and rattling is a way to call in our helping spirits. There are also longer drumming tracks that you can choose from: a twenty-minute double-drumming track and a thirty-minute single-drumming track. I recommend that you experiment with each track to see which amount of time feels the most comfortable for you.

Making a Drum or Rattle

It is easy to make a rattle using ordinary household materials. If you take some corn kernels or small stones and place them in a container, they make a great rattle. You want to work with materials whose sounds are pleasing to you and not harsh to your ears. I like the sound of corn kernels, and many of my rattles at home are filled with corn. However, in a pinch, I will use a bottle of Advil or a bottle of vitamins, whose sound is just as effective for supporting my journey. You can also go out into nature and find things with which to make your rattle or drum—in fact, anything can be made sacred with intention.

If you do decide to buy a drum or rattle, you want to look for a sound that is pleasing to you and supports you in going into an altered state of consciousness. Some people like a low tone and some people like a higher tone. All drums and rattles sound different, so be sure to try them out before buying them.

Climate changes can dramatically affect the sound of a drum that is made from animal skin. For instance, humidity will make the drum skin loose, and you will not get a clear sound. Traditionally, shamans used a ceremonial fire to dry the drum when the skin would be too loose to produce a good sound. A modern solution is to use a hair dryer to dry the drum skin. If your climate is hot and dry and the skin tightens, the sound will be very high pitched. In this case, finding some way to humidify the skin is important.

The drum I used for the drumming on the enclosed CD is a Remo drum, which is made out of FiberSkin. This type of material stays consistent in any climate. Since Remo drums are not made of animal skins, they are also suitable for people who have philosophical reasons for not wanting an animal-skin drum. Although my drum is made out of a synthetic material, it still has a strong spirit that truly comes alive when I am drumming.

I recommend that you experiment with different rhythms and different speeds of drumming or rattling to see what facilitates the strongest journey for you. For instance, some people find that they need a slower beat, or else they feel as if they are rushing in their journeys. If you find a rhythm or speed that supports you better than the drumming I have provided, you can record your own drumming to use while you journey. I also suggest that you experiment with the differences between listening to the drumming CD using speakers or headphones. Sometimes people report that one or the other helps them drop into their bodies and focus more effectively.

The drumming can be quite relaxing, and you might find yourself drifting into sleep if you start the journey when you are too tired to concentrate. If you do fall asleep while you are journeying, there is no danger involved—in fact, you will only wake up feeling refreshed!

Returning from Your Journey

You do not want to be "shocked" out of your journey. However, the fact is that our surroundings are often noisy, and we have to learn how to work with that. I have trained myself not to be distracted by the sounds that occur around me when I journey. In fact, I choose to go deeper into my journey whenever I hear a noise so that I do not experience the noise as an obstacle. If I do become shocked out of a journey and feel disoriented, I focus my attention on the drumming and return to where I was in the journey.

Returning from a journey has to do with pure will, intention, and choice. You can always take another journey at another time if you did not finish getting all the information you needed or if you want to visit another realm in non-ordinary reality.

During the drumming, I will not be speaking to you at any point. However, there will be a change in the drumbeat that will be your signal that it is time to return. If you want to return before the return signal, simply say "thank you" and "goodbye" to whomever you are in dialogue with and retrace your steps back. See or experience yourself returning via the same route, jumping off point, or entryway that you initially used to enter non-ordinary reality. Come back into the room where you are lying down or sitting and take off your headphones or turn off the drumming CD. You do not have to wait for the signal to return; however, many people like having the return beat played out for them.

The signal to return begins with four sets of seven short beats. Again, say "thank you" and "goodbye" to whomever you are talking to. Even if you are not with a helping spirit, say "thank you" and "goodbye." The reason for this is that "goodbye" signals to your psyche that something has ended. Saying "goodbye" will help you feel more grounded when you return from your journey. Remember that a shaman journeys into non-ordinary reality and back into ordinary reality with concentration and discipline.

After the change in drumbeat of four sets of seven short beats, you will hear a rapid drumbeat for about a minute. During this rapid drumbeat, retrace your steps back to your starting place and into the room where you are lying or sitting. You will then hear a second series of seven short beats, indicating that your journey is over. Take off your eye cover if you were using one, open your eyes, and turn off the CD.

After quietly reflecting on your journey, you might wish to take notes about your experience. The most important advice I can give to you is to be patient with the process and be compassionate toward yourself. I have never met a person who could not journey. However, I have met many people who tried journeying many times before they felt that something was happening. I suggest that you keep up the practice—relax, keep breathing into your heart, open all of your senses beyond just your visual awareness, set an intention, and in time, you will be journeying.

Unfortunately, we live in a culture based on immediate gratification. However, shamanic journeying is a lifelong spiritual practice that has no destination—there is no place where you should be after only a few journeys, or even after a lifetime of journeying. Once I had the opportunity to meet an Ulcchi shaman from Siberia when he came to the United States to work with a group of students. He was in his nineties when I met him, and he had begun journeying at the age of seventeen. He still called himself "a baby" in the work. This is a perfect example of a genuine shaman's attitude toward the work of shamanic journeying that we have begun.

One final warning: Please do not listen to the drumming on the enclosed CD while you are driving!

Common Questions about Shamanic Journeying

Will I experience my journeys with all of my senses?

You will find as you begin your journeys that one or two of your senses will be stronger in non-ordinary reality. Some people are more clairvoyant, meaning that they see scenes, pictures, and symbols in their journeys. Others are more clairaudient, meaning that they hear messages from their helping spirits in the form of words or voices. Others are more clairsentient—they feel the information in their bodies. And many people are some combination of the above. In my case, I am mostly clairaudient, and I largely rely on the telepathic messages that I receive from my helping spirits. I also see, feel, smell, and taste in my journeys, although these sensations are less pronounced.

In shamanic literature, you will often find the term "shamanic seeing." Shamans see with their hearts and not through their eyes. Likewise, the spirits make contact with us through our hearts, not our minds. However, due to the sheer volume of movies, TV, and computers in our culture, we have become very visually focused. As a result, one of my greatest challenges when I teach journeying is to get people to stop expecting to see their journeys as if they were watching something on TV or at the movies. Imagine never hearing voices, music, or the sounds of nature. Imagine never smelling fragrances, tasting your food, or having the ability to touch and feel others. Life becomes very rich when all of our senses are engaged, and the same is true in our shamanic journeys. Unfortunately, people in my workshops sometimes do not think they are journeying unless they are having a visual experience. So I work hard to encourage them to awaken all of their senses when they are in non-ordinary reality.

My experience is that the sense that is strongest for many people in ordinary reality is the weakest in non-ordinary reality. For example, I find that many artists do not visualize their journeys—instead, they get most of their information through feeling or hearing. Although this may be different from what they expected, the gift is that the sense that is less developed in ordinary reality suddenly has an opportunity to become enlivened and strengthened through journeying.

Part of the challenge when you begin to journey is to discover which senses are your strongest in non-ordinary reality and to trust your experience of your journeys—even if they contradict your expectations. Once you have been journeying for a while, you will find that you will see, hear, feel, taste, and smell in your journeys just like you do in your ordinary life. In addition, your intuitive abilities in ordinary reality become heightened because your senses are so engaged (and therefore, become more honed) in the course of journeying. In other words, you will develop your own unique language in journeying that may not be how you experience ordinary reality, although the benefits of it will spill over into your regular life.

There are also different styles of journeying. Some people experience themselves as meeting with or walking with their helping spirits on a journey. Some people experience themselves as being outside of the journey and watching themselves within it, as if it were a movie. And some people experience themselves merged with their power animal or teacher, moving through the journey in a merged state, rather than being separate. This is a powerful way of being on a journey, as we have joined with the power of the universe when we merge with our power animal, guardian spirit, or teacher. This is also a very healing experience. Most of us find that we flip back and forth between different styles of interaction, depending on the nature of the journey and our level of experience.

It is also important to remember that everything that happens in a journey is part of the answer to your question. You want to be aware of your surroundings—whether you see, hear, feel, smell, or taste them. Many people only focus on the answers that their power animals and teachers give them, but the weather in your journey can also be part of an answer to your question. Even where the sun is in the sky and whether it is night or day can be a part of the answer to your question.

How do our helping spirits communicate with us?

There are different ways in which the spirits communicate information to us in our shamanic journeys. One way is through telepathic messages. You might see or feel yourself with your power animal, guardian spirit, or teacher, and you might hear a message, although you do not see their lips moving. Or the spirits might show you symbols as a response to your question. Or they might take you somewhere to witness a scene that somehow answers your question. But the most common way in which the helping spirits communicate with us is through metaphor, which is a teaching method common to all spiritual traditions.

An example of this is in the Aramaic language—the language of Jesus—which was highly metaphorical and poetic. When the Bible was translated from Aramaic into Greek and then into English, the metaphors were translated literally, often changing the meaning of the words. One example is that there is no word in the Aramaic language for either "good" or "evil." The most comparable words in Aramaic were "ripe" and "unripe," referring to how everything is part of an ongoing, organic process. But when the Bible was translated into Greek and then English, the words chosen to represent "ripe" and "unripe" were "good" and "evil." This mistranslation alone shaped the evolution of Judeo-Christian culture such that human nature became perceived as something separate from the natural cycles of readiness and unreadiness.

When an answer is given literally, there is only one road to walk down. But when the spirits communicate using metaphor, there are many possible levels of teaching and meaning. I feel that the spirits are trying to inspire us to expand our perceptions of ourselves and our situations by offering guidance in this way. In addition, metaphors and poetry weave together many layers, which teaches us how everything is interconnected.

Years ago I had a powerful experience in a journey that taught me the importance of metaphoric language. I had journeyed to my power animal and asked him what I needed in my life. He told me I should garden more. I thought his answer was a bit strange, because I was traveling a lot at the time and I also lived on land that was not very fertile. But I spent a few months that summer in between my travels gardening when I could.

At the end of the summer, I suddenly realized that I had been mistaken to interpret his answer literally. It finally dawned on me that he meant for me to relate to the image of a garden as a metaphor, and to look at how I was nurturing the garden of my life and body. He was also asking me to consider how I was teaching and working with clients. Was I planting seeds of love, hope, and inspiration in my lectures and classes? Or was I planting seeds of fear? He was asking me to view all of my words as seeds, and to consider what kinds of plants were growing out of my words.

The next time I journeyed to him, he said that he was wondering how long it would take for me to understand the true meaning of his guidance. On the other hand, he observed that my real-life gardening was good for me—so it was not a complete waste of time! However, he explained that in the original journey, he was trying to offer a broader picture of my life than the postage-stamp-sized garden outside of my house. He was trying to show me that many people are filled with fear and despair, which underscores the importance of telling stories that inspire love and hopefulness. Traditionally, shamans were the psychologists of their communities—they knew the stories that would heal their clients. My power animal was asking me to make sure that I was telling healing stories to everyone I met in my classes, my practice, and my life— which was a valuable lesson.

My experience has been that our helping spirits are always trying to get us to expand and grow. They are always trying to inspire us to make positive changes and to live full and meaningful lives. They are always trying to wake us up from being disconnected from nature and the invisible worlds, since so many of us are stuck in the limiting beliefs of ordinary reality. One technique that they use is metaphor, which makes us stretch in the process of interpretation. Metaphors make us break out of the tiny boxes we put ourselves into with literal interpretations and ask us to see the bigger picture of our lives. I would still be out in my garden toiling away if I had not reflected more deeply on my guidance.

How should I language the questions that I ask my helping spirits?

My experience has been that there are two key factors to a successful journey: generating a strong intention and asking the right questions. The best kinds of questions to ask begin with the words who, what, where, or how.

When you first begin to journey, it is best to ask one question per journey. Be sure that your question does not have an "and" or an "or" in it, which would make it two questions in one. You see, if your helping spirits give you symbolic answers, you will not know what question they are answering. You might think your helping spirit has finished answering the first part and gone on to the second, when it might actually be giving you more information in response to your first question. Until you become accustomed to your shared language with your helping spirits, it is best to ask one question per journey. You can always journey again at another time to ask another question.

As you gain more experience, you might find that you can ask more than one question per journey. At this point, I am very comfortable with the form of communication that my helping spirits use, which enables me to carry on long conversations with them. However, it will take time and practice for you to reach that level.

When you are asking for help about an important decision, it is best to ask questions that will result in the most information possible. A simple yes or no answer will not help you think through a difficult decision. Likewise a "should I" or "should I not" question is not ideal. For instance, it is very common for people to ask their helping spirits whether they should marry someone. If you present that question in "should I" form, your power animal might answer, "Yes," giving the impression that the marriage will be a happy one. Later, if you have a painful marriage that does not succeed, you will wonder why you were guided to enter into it. However, your helping spirits may have viewed the marriage as an opportunity to learn important—albeit painful—lessons. It is important to understand that while our helping spirits will protect us from harm, they will not protect us from the hard lessons that we sometimes need to learn in this lifetime. On the other hand, if you had asked, "What will I learn or experience if I marry this person?" your power animal might have replied, "You will learn about betrayal." That response would have provided you with a much clearer understanding of what would unfold in your marriage—and whether or not you wanted to choose that path.

During one of my more memorable journeys, I encountered my teacher Isis who asked, "Do you know what your problem is?" I was very surprised by such an abrupt question and replied, "No. What is my problem?" She replied, "You just do not see life as an adventure."

So I told her that I had some pretty serious concerns that might be getting in the way of me feeling adventurous about life. I shared a list of concerns with her, including the fear that I might end up as a homeless person in New York City. Growing up in New York, this has always been an underlying worry of mine that my friends love to tease me about.

She looked at me and then turned away. Then she looked back at me and stared straight into my eyes and said, "What an amazing adventure that would be!"

If you think about it, it would be an adventure, but maybe not one that I would voluntarily choose. However, her view was typical of the view of spirits in non-ordinary reality—they see human life as a beautiful adventure filled with opportunities to learn and grow that can be found in even the most unexpected circumstances.

"Why" questions are sometimes fine, although they may not always be answered directly. For example, if you ask a question such as "Why did my loved one have to die in that accident?" you may not receive a clear answer. Some things belong to the mystery of life and either cannot be answered or may not be appropriate for you to understand. This certainly does not mean you cannot ask "why" questions. It is simply important to understand that there are sometimes limitations to the answers you will receive to those questions.

It is also very difficult to get accurate answers for "when" questions. Remember that you are traveling outside of time; time takes on a different and often mysterious meaning in non-ordinary reality. This is why prophecies are often inaccurate or unclear around timing, which can also be true of the answers you get to questions about when something will happen.

How do I interpret my journeys?

Although some messages are obvious and direct, journeys are often filled with symbols that can be difficult to decipher. Since shamanism is a system of direct revelation, no one can interpret your journeys except for you.

If you are stuck on the meaning of a symbol or metaphor, here are some suggestions. Try asking more questions about what occurred during the journey to see if any new information arises. For example, "How did the presence of the sun pertain to my question?" or "How did the landscape that I perceived relate to my question?" Work with each of the clear elements that were present in your journey to uncover how they provide additional information in response to your question. Another useful technique is to write in your journal or talk aloud in a stream of consciousness until your psyche reveals the answer. Often, the process of reflecting on the information given to you brings about clarity. I also recommend that when you feel stuck, journey to your helping spirits to give you the information you need in another form that might be easier for you to understand.

Am I making up my journeys?

The most common challenge that people new to the practice of shamanic journeying face is the fear that they are making up their journeys—that it is all happening in their imaginations and is therefore irrelevant.

Most of you reading this book have been raised in a society where you were taught that invisible realms do not exist. You were taught that only what you can see, feel, hear, taste, and smell is real, and the rest exists solely in your imagination. After all these years of basing your perception of reality on what is tangible, to hear someone tell you that you can travel to non-ordinary reality and ask invisible spirit beings for advice and guidance is confusing at best. This question comes up for almost everybody when they first begin the practice of shamanic journeying.

As children, many of us took great comfort in our ability to communicate with loving and caring beings in invisible worlds. However, as we grew up and became socialized into believing solely in physical reality, our relationship with the invisible world dissolved.

However, many of us yearn to rediscover the invisible worlds and our interconnectedness with all seen and unseen beings. On a profound level, we all know there is more to life than material possessions, what society tells us is true, or what we experience with our five senses.

Several years ago I was teaching an introductory workshop in journeying where the question of the imagination was very pronounced. Over and over again people asked me in different ways, "Am I making up my journey?" During a break, a Brazilian woman came up to me to tell me how surprised she was that so many people were plagued by this question. She had grown up in a culture where there is a strong belief in spirits, and for her there was no question as to whether spirits were "real." However, my parents certainly did not talk about power animals and helping spirits at the dinner table when I was growing up—nor did most of the parents of the workshop participants!

My experience has shown me that the best way to evaluate the validity of your shamanic journeys in on the basis of your results. If you keep up the practice of shamanic journeying, you will begin to see useful and beneficial results arising from the guidance you receive. Remember, shamanism has traditionally been a results-oriented system, and it is important for you to evaluate your results on an ongoing basis. The important question to ask yourself is, "Do I get information that makes a positive difference in my life?"

When you begin to see significant results, your mind will begin to quiet down, and eventually you will find that you are no longer distracted by the question of whether or not it is all happening in your imagination. However, if you try to battle your mind or beliefs while you are journeying, you will spend much of your journey time in internal dialogue and be too distracted to receive any clear information. What I do when my analytical mind interferes when I am journeying is to simply agree with what it has to say, and then continue on my journey. And what I recommend to you is that you give journeying an opportunity to reveal its benefits to you over time, which will satisfy your discerning mind.

People in our culture often forget to "lighten up" when doing spiritual practice. We tend to take everything too seriously, putting too much pressure on ourselves. Traditional shamans and healers are always laughing. Being overly serious in our journeys and lives disconnects us from our own creative potential. Learn to laugh at yourself and have fun with your practice. You will find as you journey over time that your helping spirits have quite a sense of humor and are always trying to get you to lighten up.

When I first started journeying, my power animal would find humorous settings to teach me about asking appropriate questions. I remember in one journey I went to the Lower World to meet him. When I showed up in the pine forest where he lives, he was dressed in a fancy waiter's uniform, wearing spotless white gloves. He showed me to a small round table that was decorated with a crisp white tablecloth and a small vase of flowers. He pulled out a chair for me and handed me a menu. I opened the menu and was surprised to see what was inside. There were two columns containing different questions. My power animal announced that the question I was intending to ask was the wrong one. I had not even told him what my question was, so obviously he was tuned into my intention before I even spoke it. He then explained that the questions on the menu were appropriate questions to ask, and that I could choose one question from column A and one from column B to ask him during my journey. I think this is a wonderful example of how the spirits can teach us through humor and playfulness, which helps keeps the practice more lighthearted.

What challenges might I encounter in my journey practice?

Many people get caught up in the question, "Am I journeying correctly?" Remember, there is no right way to journey—whatever you experience is correct for you. It is important to learn to honor and validate your unique experiences. This may take some time and patience, but the rewards are great.

Another common challenge is the need to see a journey visually—rather than by using our other senses. The way to work with this is to consciously open all of your senses in non-ordinary reality. If you are not seeing anything visually, simply notice what you are hearing, feeling, smelling, or tasting, and relax into receiving information in a new way.

I mentioned earlier how people in our culture tend to interpret everything that happens in a journey literally. This can change the entire meaning of the journey. Look for the metaphors. Expand your awareness to include the big picture your helping spirits are trying to show you.

One of the biggest complaints shamanic journeyers have is that they cannot stop their mind chatter while they are journeying. Often when we take time out for doing spiritual work, our mind challenges us with endless distractions. You might end up thinking about what you are going to wear to work, or what you are going to eat, or making mental lists of all the things you should be doing instead.

Repeating the intention of the journey over and over again will put you back into the journey and refocus your mind. I also suggest that you find times of the day to journey when your mind is quiet, rather than filled with distractions. Again, I suggest that you try doing some dancing or singing before you journey to quiet your mind and put you in the right heart-space for journeying.

Another way of stilling the mind is to engage in a physical activity—such as dancing or singing your journeys while they are taking place. Personally, I like to rattle for myself and sing my journeys out loud. In order to bypass the chatter of my mind, I simply drum for myself, which seems to take me deeper into my journeys. In traditional shamanic cultures, the shaman often performs his or her journey for the community by dancing, singing, or reciting aloud everything that occurs. The shaman will narrate where the group is traveling, what spirits they are meeting, what messages are being communicated, and what healing work is being done. You might also try free movement or dance while you are journeying, rather than lying down or sitting still, if that helps you focus on your journey.

When should I journey?

It is best to journey when you have a clear question or when you need help. When people first start to journey, they often become very excited about the practice and want to journey constantly. However, I would caution that you do not want to create a practice based on asking numerous questions, taking notes, but not actually applying any of the guidance in your life. In other words, you do not want to collect spiritual information and not integrate any of it into your life.

How often you should journey will become clear over time—and may be cyclical. You will sometimes find that you need more time between journeys to integrate the information, whereas at other times you will integrate the information more quickly and be ready for your next journey almost immediately.

When it comes to a particular emotional or physical issue, you may need to journey several times before you notice a change. And if you are not getting positive results around the issue, you may need to seek outside help. Sometimes when you are too emotionally attached to the outcome of an issue, you may not be able to move yourself out of the way sufficiently to access clear spiritual guidance. The same holds true if you are in an emotional state about a loved one or family member. In these cases, you would need to find someone you trust who can journey on your behalf.

I journey a lot when I am writing or working on a creative project. My helping spirits are a continuing source of inspiration to me while I write. I recommend that you try journeying when you are working on a specific project to ask for a helping spirit who is willing to support you with your project.

It is also important to be aware that you will go through many cycles with your journey practice. There might be weeks and months when your journeys are strong and clear. And then you might hit a cycle when you attempt a journey and you do not perceive any sensory information at all. This is normal—and it can last for several weeks or months. We are all a part of nature, and these are natural cycles that we are subject to. In our culture we always want to be "on." We no longer honor the incredible gestation cycle that is necessary for the regeneration that brings new life. Plants do not flower 365 days a year. In this same way, sometimes we are in a deep process of germination and gestation. During these times typically we can still journey for others, but for ourselves the curtains might close for a while. If this happens, it is important not to get frustrated or feel that your helping spirits have deserted you. They are still helping you in invisible ways. Keep journeying and checking in from time to time. Eventually your journeys will resume and become strong and clear once again.

How do I know when I should go to the Lower World or the Upper World?

I find that when people learn to journey, they are often more attracted to one world than the others. Some people have an easier time journeying to the Lower World and find it harder to get into the Upper World. Some people have the opposite experience. Many people are comfortable journeying in both worlds. This often changes over time, depending on what you are working on. Your style of journeying will evolve, and the worlds that you feel most comfortable with will change. It is important to stay flexible.

With experience, you will find that your power animals and teachers specialize in different areas. You will learn which helping spirits to ask in regards to different kinds of questions and help. In my own practice, my power animal is usually available for my clients and for me, although my teachers tend to offer the best information related to my writing and broader global issues. Many shamanic practitioners work with their teachers in human form when working with clients. Through journeying on a regular basis, you begin to identify which power animal or teacher to go to for certain types of questions or issues. You will find that different helping spirits have different specialties. Even when your helping spirits have demonstrated specialties, it is fine to journey to different spirits to ask their opinions on the same issue—they will often have different and valuable perspectives to share with you.

Remember that your power animals and teachers may change over time. They may stay with you for years, or you may find that new helping spirits present themselves to you when you ask for different types of help.

During your journeys, you can move between the worlds as much as you like. If you are journeying to the Lower World, and you want to be in the Upper World, simply make your way up. Similarly, you can travel from the Upper World down into the Lower World if you wish. Your power animals and teachers can travel in between all three worlds, so there is no limit to where you can go and whom you can meet.

Look for the surprise element in your journeys. You will often find spirits volunteering to help you whose identities will surprise you. You will get answers and help in ways that are unexpected. The element of surprise in my journeys is largely what has kept me so engaged in my shamanic practice for the last twenty years.

Think of your shamanic journeying practice as a work in progress. It will deepen and grow in proportion to how much time you devote to it. The key is continuing to practice and developing a trusting relationship with your helping spirits. This will happen naturally with time.

Allow your journeys to be fluid and organic. Explore different levels in both directions. Be open to meeting new helping spirits who can be of assistance to you. Be an adventurer! Take in the love, wisdom, and healing that your helping spirits and the universe are longing to share with you.

Undertaking Your First
Shamanic Journey

I n this chapter I will summarize three journeys. I suggest you try them one by one to begin your journeying practice.

Journeying to the Lower World

Your first journey will be to the Lower World to meet and develop a relationship with your power animal.

Begin by seeing yourself in a location in nature that you have visited in ordinary reality where there is a natural opening into the earth. This can be a tree trunk with deep roots into the earth, the center of a volcano, a hole in the ground, an opening in a cave, or through a body of water such as a lake, stream, river, or waterfall. As I mentioned before, if it works best for you to see yourself traveling down on an elevator or through an underground subway tunnel, that is also fine.

See yourself entering into the opening, where you will find yourself in a transitional space of some kind—generally a tunnel. Follow the tunnel until you reach the light, and when you come out into the Lower World, notice the landscape around you and see if there is an animal close by.

If an animal is there, ask it, "Are you my power animal?" Asking a simple yes or no question will give you immediate insight into how your power animal wants to communicate with you. Your power animal may respond telepathically, or it may lead you somewhere or show you something that holds a message for you. If this is your power animal, begin building a relationship with him or her by asking a question or asking for a tour of that level of the Lower World. For example, you could begin by asking what teaching that particular animal brings you that will be of benefit to you. Or, if the animal is not your power animal, continue on your journey until you locate the animal that is.

Try to stay in the journey with your power animal until you hear the drum calling you back. Or, if you wish to come back before the return beat, retrace your steps back to the room where you are lying or sitting, open your eyes, and stop the CD.

If your experience differs from my directions in any way, follow your experience and disregard my directions. For instance, some people find that they bypass the tunnel and just arrive in the Lower World. Or you might meet a teacher instead of a power animal in the Lower World. Do not restrict your journeys by trying to conform to my directions. They are simply intended to provide a general guideline for you as you begin this practice. Allow yourself to move with your unique experience while it is happening.

To visit deeper levels of the Lower World, look for new openings in the earth that will take you to further depths. There are many levels farther down in the Lower World and farther up in the Upper World. Just like when you began, you can keep traveling down by finding new entrances in the earth and descending from one level to the next.

Journeying to the Middle World

Before you begin your journey to the Middle World, make sure you have a clear intention and purpose for your journey. When you journey in the Middle World, you are traveling within the landscape of your physical reality, although your experience may be quite different from when you simply walk out your front door. First, you will be encountering the invisible spirits of the beings that share your environment, such as the spirits of land, rocks, animals, trees, and plants. Second, you will be able to travel very quickly through space, rather than being limited by your physical body.

For a journey in the Middle World, see yourself walking out your front door and traveling through physical reality to locate a lost object or perhaps to visit a place with which you would like to commune. You can learn a great deal by communicating with the spirits of nature in a Middle World journey, as well as the elements of water, air, earth, and fire.

You can also journey to the sun, the stars, and the other planets in our solar system, each of which has much to teach you about how to restore balance and live in alignment with your natural cycles. In the Middle World, we also have access to the fairies, devas, and elves, who are collectively known as the spirit people. There are also guardians of the forest that you can meet. In sum, important journeys to the Middle World are those that enable us to discover the spirits of the invisible beings who are around us all the time, but whom we may not perceive in ordinary reality.

When you hear the return beat, retrace your steps back into the room where you are lying or sitting, open your eyes, and turn off the CD. Or, if you wish to conclude your journey before you hear the return beat, simply retrace your steps back into the room where you are journeying, open your eyes, and turn off the CD.

Journeying to the Upper World

Your first journey to the Upper World will be for the purpose of meeting a teacher in human form.

With that intention in mind, begin by seeing yourself at a particular location in nature that will help you travel upward. For example, you can see yourself climbing up a tree, rope, or ladder, jumping from the top of a mountain, rising up on a tornado or a whirlwind, climbing over a rainbow, going up with the smoke of a fire or through a chimney, or finding a bird to take you up. You may also ask your power animal to carry you up. Any way that you can get to the Upper World is fine.

You will pass through a transition—such as a cloud or a layer of fog—that will indicate that you have entered the Upper World. When you have passed through the transition, you will arrive in the first level of the Upper World. If you are still seeing planets and stars as you journey upward, you have not yet reached the Upper World. Again, you will know that you are in the Upper World because of the sensation of having passed through a permeable threshold of some kind, after which the landscape will change.

Notice if there is a teacher waiting there to greet you. If so, ask, "Are you my teacher?" If you get an affirmative answer or gesture, ask your teacher a question that is important to you, such as for healing help for an emotional or physical issue. You can also ask your teacher to show you around the Upper World. If your teacher is not waiting for you at the first level, keep searching through the different levels of the Upper World until you find someone who says that he or she is your teacher.

You can also keep traveling to higher levels by looking around for a means of going higher up—notice what appears to you as a means of transportation. As with your power animal, the initial conversation with your teacher will reveal how he or she communicates with you and what gifts he or she brings to you.

When you hear the return beat, retrace your steps back into the room you are journeying in, open your eyes, and turn off the CD. Or, if you wish to conclude your journey before you hear the return beat, simply retrace your steps back into the room where you are lying down or sitting, open your eyes, and turn off the CD.

Please note: Power animals and teachers in human form live in both the Lower and Upper Worlds. After you have completed your first journeys, you can reverse the process. You can find a teacher in human form in the Lower World or go to meet a power animal in the Upper World.

Divination and
Healing Journeys

Divination Journeys

One of the traditional roles of a shaman was to divine information for individuals and the community at large. Some shamanic practitioners still divine information for clients and the communities they live in, although many do not feel called to journey on behalf of others. Instead, they use shamanic journeying to access guidance about their own issues. Your helping spirits are a wonderful resource when it comes to answering questions pertaining to your relationships, health issues, or work issues. You can also ask for information that can help you grow and evolve in a broader sense. For instance, you can ask a question like, "What do I need to focus on in my life right now?"

Here are some other examples of questions to inspire divination journeys:

- How can I heal my body?
- How can I heal my relationship?
- Show me my new life (if you are going through a transition).
- How can I prepare for...?
- What can I do to resolve the tension in my family and work environment?
- How can I be of help to a loved one, a friend, an animal, or the land I live on? (Choose only one at a time.)
- Where should I look for a house?
- Please help me find a new job.
- What will I learn if I make this choice?
- What is the root cause of my fear? (Or you can choose another life issue.)

To divine information in a journey, begin with a clear question that you would like to ask one of your helping spirits. Decide which of your helping spirits you would like to have answer your question, and journey to the place where you normally meet him or her. Of course, you can ask your question to more than one of your helping spirits. Simply find them in their usual places in non-ordinary reality and ask as many of them as you wish to answer your question. This is what is known as a divination journey.

In the past, I have had terrible luck buying used cars, and I was always visiting a mechanic. When I learned how to journey, I would go to my power animal and ask him for a diagnosis of the mechanical problem before going to the mechanic. My mechanic knew I had no knowledge of cars.

At the time I could not even put gas in the car without help. The first time I showed up telling my mechanic what I thought was wrong, he just laughed at me. When I picked up my car after he had fixed it, he said with amazement, "You were right!"

This continued over time. Each time I brought my car in, I presented a diagnosis, and each time my diagnosis was correct. Finally my mechanic asked me what I was doing to find out the problems with my car. I was shy about actually saying I took a shamanic journey and that my power animal would slide under the car on a trolley to perform diagnostic tests. I finally did break down and tell him that I practiced shamanic journeying and my power animal provided me with the information I needed. After that, whenever I brought my car in, my mechanic would first always ask me what my power animal had told me about the problem.

Barbara had a friend who made a clear decision to leave her husband. Her friend asked Barbara to journey on the question, "Where should I go after I leave my husband?" Barbara saw her in an area surprisingly close to where she presently lived, so she asked someone else to journey on the same question. The second practitioner received the same response as Barbara had, so Barbara asked her friend to reconsider her decision to leave her husband. Her friend chose to work things through with her husband, and they now have a healthy relationship.

After a great deal of experience with journeying, some people choose to use shamanic journeys to access information for friends, clients, and their communities. However, before making yourself available in this way, you must be certain that you are getting good results from your own shamanic journeys. Remember, if shamans were not able to successfully divine food sources for their communities or provide healing for their fellow tribes-people, their community would not survive. The practice of shamanism has always been based on practical and accurate results.

If you have reached a level where you would like to journey to ask for guidance on behalf of your friends, family, or community members, please consider the following ethical issues. First, it is vital that you have permission to journey for someone else. We live in a culture that encourages us to try to help people whether they want it or not. Instead, I believe that we need to respect each other's choices—how each of us individually learns, heals, and grows. People do not heal or grow until they are ready for it. It does not work to push healing onto others. Information is a form of healing, so please wait until someone asks for your help before interfering in his or her life. In order for a successful healing to take place, the person must be ready to receive healing.

In addition, if you are having a problem with someone at work or someone you are in relationship with, it is not appropriate to journey and ask, "What is this person's problem?" This would be looking into someone's life without permission—a form of non-ordinary spying. Instead, I would undertake a journey and ask the question, "How can I heal this relationship? What behavior or perceptual change do I need to make in order to heal this situation? What is the lesson for me to learn?" The key to a successful journey is to keep the focus on yourself, rather than looking at what is happening for someone else—unless they have asked you.

There is an exception to this rule that is important to clarify. When I was a practicing psychotherapist seeing clients, I would occasionally use shamanic journeying to assist my diagnosis. For example, if I felt that the client and I were dancing around the core issues without being able to identify them and make progress, I would ask my power animal to identify the underlying issues. In this situation, my clients were coming to see me to receive my help—and they expected me to use all of the tools in my toolbox in order to best help them. Therefore, within the context of the helping professions, I believe that it is ethical to use journeying as a diagnostic tool. However, analyzing someone in non-ordinary reality when they have not asked for your help is not considered appropriate.

Finally, you also do not want to ask the helping spirits to send healing—in any form—to someone who has not asked for it. Once again, it is important to maintain appropriate boundaries and decorum around your shamanic practice.

Healing Journeys

In traditional shamanic cultures, the shaman addressed the spiritual dimension of illness by intervening in non-ordinary reality on behalf of his or her clients. In those instances, the client did not journey for himself or herself.

However, since many of us now have access to our own helping spirits using shamanic journeying, it is worthwhile to ask your power animal or teacher to perform a healing on you when you need it. The healing could take any number of forms, depending on the nature of the issue and the way your helping spirit works.

To do a healing journey, begin with a clear idea of the issue or ailment that is in need of healing. Decide which of your helping spirits you would like to ask to receive a healing from and journey to where you normally meet them in non-ordinary reality. You may find that whomever you ask will not provide the healing themselves, but may take you to another helping spirit who is more skilled in this way.

For instance, Larry was having stomach problems. He could not digest his food and was in great pain. He went to doctors who could not find the source of his problem. He journeyed to his teacher, who was his great-grandfather, and asked for help. His teacher asked him to lie down on the floor of his house. At first Larry felt like he was floating, and then he was flooded with unconditional love and light and felt a peace that he had never felt before. When he returned from his journey, he felt pain-free for the first time in months. He took a series of journeys to discover how he could maintain his health on a long-term basis. Since then he has followed directions and advice given to him by his great-grandfather and continues to live a healthy life.

Since shamanism works with the spiritual aspect of illness, it can also be combined with traditional medical and psychological treatment. In many indigenous cultures, shamans and physicians work together to provide treatment.

Connie was diagnosed with breast cancer. She chose to have a lumpectomy and radiation, as advised by her doctors. Combined with her traditional medical treatment, she journeyed to hummingbird and asked for help. She combined her shamanic work with dreamwork. Hummingbird instructed Connie to make breast casts and paint them with healing images. And then within a week she was given a grant to teach workshops on this healing method to women who have been diagnosed with breast cancer.

Dale worked in a manufacturing plant where he could not get along with another worker. He journeyed and asked his power animal what he could do. He was told to get two stones and paint them two different colors and keep them in his pocket. He did this and without any other intervention the problems with his coworker cleared up in a very short time. This is an example of how a mysterious ritual that cannot be analyzed with our rational minds can create change and healing.

A dismemberment in a journey is a classic means of spiritual healing. An animal like a bear or eagle, or a force of nature such as wind, takes your body apart down to the bone. What is ill is taken out, and you are rebuilt again with healthy body parts. It is very common to receive a dismemberment when asking for a healing. Although it might sound gruesome, people report a tremendous amount of peace and love during the experience.

For instance, Susan's heart was hurting over the loss of a family member, and so she journeyed to her power animal,

which is a horse, for healing. Horse called on bear to perform a dismemberment. Bear ripped her apart and took
out her heart, and then put her back together with a heart
that was healed. Susan felt great relief after this journey.

Dismemberment journeys can also be understood as a person being initiated into a spiritual path. Your body and ego,
which keep you separate from the power of the universe,
is temporarily taken from you, enabling you to remember
that you are not just a body, but a spiritual being connected
to all of life. Once a person has a profound experience of
this unity, he or she often comes back from it with healing
abilities or a deeper ability to work spiritually.

If you undertake a healing journey and feel that the healing you received was beneficial, you might wish to repeat
the journey in order to deepen the results. However, if the
healing did not feel effective, you may need the help of a
healer in ordinary reality who is not so personally attached
to the outcome.

Another healing journey is to find a restful place in
the Lower World or Upper World where you can simply
de-stress from your day. This type of journey can be very
restorative. You can journey with that simple intention and
return feeling quite refreshed.

There are more advanced shamanic techniques for the
purposes of healing others that are beyond the scope of this
program. However, there are many workshops taught around
the world for those who want to learn these shamanic healing techniques. Please consult the list of resources at the
end of this program to research those options.

Additional Journeys

I have given you some ideas about journeys for divination and for personal healing. I also encourage you to meet with the spirits of animals, birds, plants, trees, rocks, insects, fish, and reptiles with whom we share this great earth. In teaching beginning workshops on shamanic journeying, participants often report that they love the practice, but that they do not know what kinds of questions or intentions to journey on. What follows is a list of additional possible topics you can explore in your shamanic journeys. Please feel free to add to this list and create your own topics for journeying.

Journeys of Interpretation

- Ask for an interpretation of a dream. You might phrase your question as "What do I need to know about my dream?"

- Ask the question: "What is the message or meaning of a symbol in my journey that I do not understand?"
- Ask the question: "What is the meaning of the omen or sign I received while I was taking a walk in nature?"
- Ask the question: "What is the lesson or gift for me in this difficult time?"

Journeys to Learn about Your History

- Ask to meet an ancestor.
- Ask to be shown the gifts and strengths of your ancestral line that you are carrying in this lifetime. Often we only focus on what we did not get from our families. Through the process of survival of the fittest, we are carrying gifts through our family lines. Be sure to look at the strengths of both your mother's and father's side of the family. This has been an especially healing journey for people who were adopted or do not know much about their ancestral roots.
- Ask to be shown a creation myth or story so you can learn how you and the world around you were created.
- Ask to meet with the spirit of a deceased loved one in the Lower or Upper World to resolve unfinished conversations with them. This is a good way to complete your feelings with someone who has passed away.

Journeys to Help Restore Harmony and Balance in Your Life after You Have Received Spiritual, Psychological, or Medical Help

- Ask the question: "What changes do I need to make in

my life in order to stay healthy over time or to support my healing process?"

- Ask the question: "How can I use my creative energy to create a positive present and future for myself?"
- Ask the question: "What would bring meaning and passion back into my life?"
- Ask the question: "What are some simple practices I can perform throughout the day to transform the energy around my anger, fear, sadness, or frustration?"
- Ask the question: "What is a personal myth or life story that no longer serves me?"

Journeys to Connect with the Natural World

- Journey to meet with the natural world.
- Journey to a crystal or other object and learn how it wants to be used.
- Journey to the spirit of the land or city where you live to meet it and learn about its energy. You can journey to the spirit of the place where you live or a place you wish to learn more about.
- Journey to the moon to learn about the moon's cycles and how they affect you.
- Journey to learn about how you are affected by different seasons.
- Journey to learn how you can schedule your life so you are in sync with the cycles of nature.
- Journey to a body of water to learn about its power.
- Journey to the stars to learn more about them.
- Journey to the spirit of insects or rodents invading your

home or garden and negotiate with them.

- Journey to learn about the weather spirits.
- Journey to meet with the spirits of earth, air, water, and fire.
- Journey to learn about the power of the sun and how its energy is necessary for all of life to thrive.

Journeys to Receive Instruction for Creating and Performing Ceremonies

- Ask for a ceremony that you can perform to release and transform fear, anger, or a block to your creativity.
- Ask for a ceremony that you can perform to help you manifest a dream or desire.
- Ask for a ceremony that you can perform to celebrate a life transition such as puberty, menopause, marriage, a move, or a change in career.
- Ask for a ceremony that you can perform for mourning or to say goodbye to a loved one.
- Ask for a ceremony that you can perform to honor someone in your family or someone with whom you work.
- Ask for a ceremony that you can perform to bring joy or health into your life.
- Ask for a ceremony that you can perform to honor the change in seasons.

Journeys for Social Issues

- Journey to ask for help in resolving a conflict with a loved one, friends, family, or coworkers.
- Journey to ask to meet with the power animal of the

business or organization where you are employed. Ask the power animal how it can help you to restore balance and harmony in the environment in which you work.

- Journey to ask for help with creative projects.
- Journey to ask to meet the power animal of your relationship or family.
- Journey to ask about the power of words and how the vibration and intention coming from the words we speak can create healing and peace.
- Journey to ask how you can help heal a social wound.
- Journey to find out how you can be of service and help heal environmental or global problems.

Journeys for Exploration

- Journey to explore and experience the landscape in different levels in the Lower World and Upper World.
- Journey to meet different helping spirits in the different levels of the Lower World or Upper World. Learn what messages or information they have to share with you.

Integrating Your Journey Practice
with Your Community

J ourney groups have formed around the world where people journey together and then share their experiences, giving people a strong sense of community and the gift of being witnessed by other journeyers. In most journey groups, the members journey on their own issues and on questions for one another. When you ask other journeyers to journey on your behalf, you will often get helpful and new information that you did not receive yourself.

Some groups journey collectively on a question, such as a question about a global issue or some aspect of current events. For example, how to address the climate changes in their community or a social issue about which they are concerned. Many groups will ask about how to honor a change in season or the current phase of the moon, or to create rituals together as a community. Each member of the group will receive a unique piece of information that can be woven together to inspire and educate the whole group. There may also be similarities and synchronicities among the answers given, which will underscore something of particular importance.

Many well-meaning journeyers report that it is hard to commit to a once-a-week journey group. The feedback I receive is that meeting twice a month works best and results in the most consistent level of attendance. I have also noticed that the groups that stay together the longest journey for each other as well as for community and global issues. These groups evolve into true communities where individual issues are addressed as well as issues that affect the entire group.

I would like to offer one warning for those who choose to journey in a group. Please do not compare the information you receive with the other group members. Sometimes this produces a feeling of envy between group members who wish their journeys were more like someone else's. It is critical to honor your own unique style of journeying—as well as each other's style—rather than deeming one style to be more advanced than the others.

If you are new to journeying, you may consider sharing this program with some friends as a way of creating a group of journeyers in your community. Then you can journey on your own and perhaps meet every two weeks to do some group journeys together.

Shamanic journeying is an incredible tool to receive healing and guidance in our lives. With the help of our spirits, we can be guided to create a life filled with meaning, joy, and passion. We begin to wake up from the spell we have been under that says we are only what we seem to be in the material world. We begin to engage in a dance with life and life's cycles. We learn to move from a life of fear and survival into one in which we begin to thrive.

You are embraced by the love of the universe and the helping spirits. Open your heart to the love, wisdom, and healing they have to share. In doing this, you can not only change your own life, but the changes in consciousness we can achieve together through shamanic journeying can transform the world as well.

Resources

For information on workshops taught by Sandra Ingerman, please either write to:

Sandra Ingerman
P.O. Box 4757
Santa Fe, NM 87502

or visit Sandra's Website:
www.sandraingerman.com.

For a list of local shamanic teachers and practitioners in your area, visit www.shamanicteachers.com.

About the Author

Sandra Ingerman, MA, is the author of *Soul Retrieval: Mending the Fragmented Self, Welcome Home: Following Your Soul's Journey Home, A Fall to Grace, Medicine for the Earth: How to Transform Personal and Environmental Toxins,* and *How to Heal Toxic Thoughts: Simple Tools for Personal Transformation.* She has recorded a three-hour lecture, *The Soul Retrieval Journey, The Beginner's Guide to Shamanic Journeying,* and *Miracles for the Earth* with Sounds True.

Sandra teaches workshops internationally on shamanic journeying, healing, and reversing environmental pollution using spiritual methods. She is recognized for bridging ancient cross-cultural healing methods to our modern culture, addressing the needs of our times. Sandra is a licensed marriage and family therapist and a professional mental health counselor.

About Sounds True

Sounds True was founded in 1985 with a clear vision: to dissemi-
nate spiritual wisdom. Located in Boulder, Colorado, Sounds
True publishes teaching programs that are designed to educate,
uplift, and inspire. We work with many of the leading spiritual
teachers, thinkers, healers, and visionary artists of our time.

To receive a free catalog of tools and teachings for personal
and spiritual transformation, please visit www.soundstrue.com,
call toll-free 800-333-9185, or write to us at The Sounds True
Catalog, P.O. Box 8010, Boulder CO 80306.